PENGUIN BOOKS

Venice

VENICE,

AN INTERIOR

JAVIER MARÍAS

Translated from the Spanish by

MARGARET JULL COSTA

PENGUIN BOOKS

PENGUIN BOOKS

UK | USA | Canada | Ireland | Australia
India | New Zealand | South Africa

Penguin is part of the Penguin Random House group of companies
whose addresses can be found at global.penguinrandomhouse.com.

First published as *Venecia, un interior* in Spain in *El País* 1988
This translation first published in the United States of
America in the *Threepenny Review* 2013
First published in the United Kingdom in Penguin Books 2016
001

Set in 11.3/17 pt Bodoni Twelve
Typeset by Jouve (UK), Milton Keynes
Text design by Davide Romualdi
Printed in Great Britain by Clays Ltd, St Ives plc

A CIP catalogue record for this book is available from the British Library

ISBN: 978-0-241-24887-4

www.greenpenguin.co.uk

Contents

The Venetians

Let us begin with what you don't see, perhaps the only thing that isn't on show, whose existence seems improbable and, to the visitor, almost impossible. People who *live* in Venice! Men and women who have nothing to do with the tourist machine and who live there *permanently*! Human beings who spend the whole year in that Great Museum, throughout the city's four long seasons! Individuals who are not content with the mere three or five or seven days that every mortal should set aside in the vast diary of his or her biography to be spent in the one place in the world that, if left unvisited, could tarnish the worthy portrait of someone who throughout his life - however decent or dissolute - has always done his aesthetic duty!

Only this threat to the perfection of our lived experience can explain why it is that, along with younger tourists (the dreaded backpackers who muddy the waters in summer), vast groups of ancient, even decrepit, visitors appear in St Mark's Square with eyes protected by cameras with dioptre lenses or else fixed firmly on the ground, as if they were afraid to look up and straight ahead and finally see what it is deemed vital that every human being on the planet should see at least once, as if looking up might bring about their own immediate departure to that other paradise from which there is no return. Indeed, sometimes the crews on the planes that land at Marco Polo Airport – with its distinctly Central American feel – won't allow the able-bodied passengers off for a good half-hour because of the large number of 'wheelchairs' (as a stewardess with a utilitarian mindset insists on calling the people occupying them) who have to be deposited on terra firma first and by the not entirely risk-free means of rudimentary cranes and plastic toboggans. An hour later, of course, the 'wheelchairs' will have to tackle the insoluble problem of climbing innumerable steps and bridges, but at least they will not have to add to their other misfortunes the

2

ignominy of never having seen Venice. You simply have to see it.

Venetians are aware of this, and the knowledge that their city is the key destination in the rest of humanity's dream geography has forged their character and determined how they view themselves in relation to the world. It's hardly surprising then that Venetians, even now, consider themselves to be the centre of that world so hell-bent on visiting them that it is prepared, if necessary, to do so on its knees. Some of the more arrogant Venetians can still be heard to say that the *campo* – the country – begins on the other side of the Ponte della Libertà, the only connection (apart from the railway bridge) between the mainland and the group of islands that make up the city. That two-mile-long bridge, the brain-child of Mussolini, Vittorio Cini and Count Volpi de Misurata, has attached the city to the peninsula for well over fifty years now, allowing cars to lay siege to Venice, at its very gates, like some new form of dragon, and the bridge is perceived by Venetians as an impertinent umbilical cord, which they have no option but to accept. For Venetians, Venice is the City par excellence. The rest of the world is merely *campo*. The harshest and most belligerent version of this idea has a racist variant: 'Blacks begin on the other side of the Ponte della Libertà.'

But these inhabitants – the only true Whites in their opinion, the only civilized people in all humanity, which they consider barbarous by comparison – are not easy to spot. Invaded, harassed, plundered, driven out and slowly deprived of their White customs and urban traditions, there are ever fewer of those who stubbornly refuse to give any more ground. Throughout the twentieth century Venetians emigrated in steadily growing numbers to Mestre, which started out as a working-class district a few miles from the city and is now the secret envy of those treacherous Venetians who have grown frail and unsteady on their feet, because it has discotheques, cinemas, young people, department stores, supermarkets, things to do, life. In the days of the Republic, Venice had almost three hundred thousand inhabitants. Now there are only seventy thousand, and the desertions are not over yet.

Venetians are not easy to spot; largely because

they don't go out very much. Entrenched behind their watermelon-green shutters, they watch the rest of the world – the periphery of the world – in their pyjamas and via their twenty TV channels. Their indifference and lack of curiosity about anything other than themselves and their ancestors has no equivalent in even the most inward-turning of villages in the northern hemisphere. Venice's three cinemas tend to be languid, half-empty places, as do the Teatro Goldoni, the bars and the streets as darkness falls, the lecture theatres and even the concert halls, although, as I will explain later, these are often the exceptions. Almost nothing will drag Venetians from their houses; almost nothing will shift them from their city. They avoid anywhere that has been developed with tourists in mind or that has in some way been contaminated by tourism, which means nearly everywhere. Their space is shrinking fast, but of course you won't see them sitting on café terraces listening to an anachronistic orchestra (clarinet, violin, double bass, grand piano and accordion) in St Mark's Square, nor in the nearby restaurants and *trattorie*, nor along the shrill, fairground-like Riva degli Schiavoni facing the lagoon, nor, needless to say, in a gondola. And they will only be seen in the ineluctable Caffè Florian at ungodly hours when any visitors are likely to be sleeping the deep sleep of the exhausted tourist. On the other hand, you might find them in places that seem unalluring to the traveller, but which are the last redoubt of the Venetians' circumscribed habits, places about which travel agents neglect to inform their already overwhelmed clientele: at midday, the Venetian ladies and gentlemen drink their aperitif in Paolin, an unassuming ice-cream-parlour-cum-bar; they take their evening stroll along the sublime Zattere; and after dark, night-owls and music-lovers can be found in the old-fashioned, hidden-away Salone Campiello, one of the few places that stays open after ten o'clock. On opera nights, of course, the locals can be found at the eighteenth-century Teatro La Fenice, the favourite meeting place of the whitest and most urbane of Venetians, that is, the proudest, most exclusive, most scornful and influential. Not that La Fenice is a particularly important theatre, nor can the operatic tradition of Venice be compared with that of Milan, but it is there, in the orchestra stalls, that the *gente per bene*, the true Venetians, go to see and be seen.

Precisely because the strictly musical function of those seats is even more reduced or attenuated than it is in most such places, they become a showcase for dresses, shoes, fur coats and jewels; and the Venetians' own ignorance of the outside world leads them to misjudge how much to display or, to be more exact, to show no judgement at all. Singers at the theatre sometimes complain that their voices cannot be heard above the rattle of jewellery and that their eyes are dazzled by the glint of gold in the darkness, because some ladies do rather over-adorn hands, ears and neck in their eagerness to outshine, well, themselves principally.

Indeed, that is one of the identifying features of the Venetians, by which I mean their need to get dressed up and put on fine clothes, shoes and jewellery. In fact, the curious traveller will probably be able to identify the few natives he may come across in his wanderings fairly easily because, just as tourists go around looking shabby, not to say downright grubby, Venetians seem always to be on their way to some elegant party at any time

7

of the day or year, even when the heat and humidity join forces to leave the most dapper dripping with sweat. You can recognize Venetian women in particular by three things: their lovely carved, chiselled, angular faces are always heavily made-up like the women in Egon Schiele paintings; they walk very fast; and they have beautiful, toned legs from a lifetime of going up and down steps and crossing bridges.

Nevertheless they're not that easy to spot. They don't even take the same streets as tourists. Driven out of the bright main thoroughfares, where the continuous flow of people occasionally causes human traffic jams that are frustrating in the extreme to those with appointments to keep, Venetians seek out short cuts and set off down byways that no foreigner would venture into for fear of becoming lost for ever in the unfathomable labyrinth that is Venice: alleys barely wide enough for one person, narrow passageways between two buildings, arcades that appear to lead nowhere, back lanes that look as if they will end up in the canal. The Venetians have been obliged to surrender their streets to incomers, to people from the *campo*, and they traverse instead a hidden Venice, parallel to that of the tourist itineraries signed with yellow arrows. In fact, they don't often get to enjoy the loveliest parts of their city, the ones that everyone else dreams of seeing: they see instead chipped and crumbling walls, tiny bridges over anonymous dwarfish canals, cracked and peeling stucco, the reverse side of the city, its shadow-self, in which there are no shops or hotels, restaurants or bars, only the essential elements, stone and water. They also avoid the crowded *vaporetti*, or waterbuses, and so are forced to walk miles whenever they leave the house. At most, they might allow themselves to take the *traghetto*, or gondola, which, for a few pence, carries them from one side of the Grand Canal to the other. This, however, also turns out to be one of the city's most thrilling experiences, for while the *traghetto* offers only a brief crossing, avoiding the *vaporetti* and the motorboats travelling up and down the canal, it affords its passengers a glimpse of the palaces from the height at which they were intended to be seen.

The archipelago

Venetians, as well those who, though not born in Venice, live here, and, indeed, even those visitors who dare to stay longer than the period stipulated by most conventional biographies, all end up losing the desire or will to leave the city. We can discuss later the real reason for this strange fixity, for the total engagement with the city felt by those who linger too long in Venice, this mixture of contentment and resignation. The fact is, though, that Venetians rarely leave their city, and when they do, it is only in order to travel somewhere that has always belonged to them anyway.

The large island of the Lido, whose beaches Visconti immortalized in that collection of picture postcards for maritime aesthetes entitled *Death in Venice*, is today, in contrast to what we were shown in the movie, a totally domestic place, and not in the least international. It's a family beach to which Venetians travel daily during the month of July, making the twenty-minute crossing over the grey waters of the lagoon. Awaiting them will be a beach hut, which, for the season, will have cost them five million lira to rent, and which they will use for that one month and the first week of September only, because in August they will be holidaying in 'their' mountains, the Dolomites. These are probably the greatest distances they will cover in the whole of their reclusive existences. The Venetians' fugitive nature even obliges them to avoid the beach of the Hotel des Bains on which Dirk Bogarde's drowsy eyes lingered so interminably. Not only do they fear that it might attract the occasional tourist made up to look like Aschenbach or coiffed à la Tadzio, they also consider it second-rate. The really good beach, they say, belongs to the Hotel Excelsior.

The Lido, in other respects, is a summer version of the orchestra stalls at La Fenice. Venetian society is so inbred that, just as its members despise all foreigners (not to mention their compatriots, especially if they're *terroni*, people who come from any city south of Rome), they admire each other immensely, and in places where they know that they're likely to meet, they do their utmost to arouse the boundless admiration of their mirror images. This is why the ladies arrive at the beach wearing designer silk dresses, strappy gold stilettos and all the diamonds, emeralds, sapphires, pearls and aqua-marines they have at their disposal. The silks and the shoes will be left in the beach hut, but the jewellery and the gold will remain even when the lady decides to take a break from social chit-chat for a moment and bathe in the warm, pale waters of the sea.

Each island in the small archipelago of which Venice forms a part seems to have or have had some specific function. Venice itself is made up of a group of islands and, before it took on the identity of a city, it was called the Rialto. Now-adays, seen from above, there appear to be only two islands, separated by the Grand Canal as if by a pair of meticulous, patient, curved scissors. Put together so that they almost fit each other, the islands look rather like a painter's palette. These two islands are not intended to serve anyone, but to be served by others. Determined that her immutable surface or face should be exposed only to the important things in life, Venice distributes about the lagoon any task or occupation or service that is deemed too specialized or too shameful, anything subsidiary, unpleasant, functional, unsavoury, anything that should not be seen and has no place in the city's administrative, ecclesiastical, courtly, nautical, commercial self.

So, for example, the island of Sant'Erasmo is the city's garden. From there and from the islands of Vignole and Mazzorbo come almost all of Venice's fruit and vegetables. Taking a boat along the canals of Vignole is like plunging into a jungle landscape. The green areas that you don't see in Venice (they do exist, but are hidden) are to be found on these island-gardens, on these island-warehouses. San Clemente and San Servolo, for their part, were home, respectively, to the insane asylums for men and women, until those institutions were abolished by the Italian state ten or fifteen years ago. San Lazzaro degli Armeni was a leper colony until the eighteenth century, when, as its name indicates, it was handed over to the large and highly cultured Armenian community, just as La Giudecca was the island chosen by the Jews (the ghetto was another matter) as a place to live. Sacca Sessola received TB patients, while on San Francesco del Deserto there is only a monastery (Franciscan of course) with immaculately kept gardens patrolled by peacocks. Burano has its speciality too: the famous *merletti*, or lace, although most of what is sold there now is made in Hong Kong and Taiwan – as is almost everything sold anywhere in the world. And Murano, where you can find the astonishing apse of Santa Maria e Donato, dating from the end of the eleventh century, is, otherwise, a succession of shops and factories making and selling hand-blown glass, the business from which the island makes its living. There they create Barovier fruit, Venini vases and Moretti wine goblets. Indeed, the whole island has a glassy stare to it.

However, the most thrilling of the islands is Torcello. There is almost nothing on Torcello: two churches, three restaurants and La Locanda Cipriani. According to Giovanna Cipriani, the grand-daughter of the founder of this exquisite chain of hotels and restaurants, St Hemingway, the patron saint of tourists, used to stay at La Locanda, existing for days on end on a diet of sandwiches and wine, large quantities of which (the wine) were taken up to him in his room. The rest of the island is barely populated and dominated by some curiously unrampant vegetation.

But Torcello is basically where Venice originated, the first island that looked likely to be inhabited permanently by refugees from Aquileia, Altino, Concordia and Padua, who built stilt-houses in the estuary in their temporary flight from the Barbarian invasions of the fifth century. Torcello was the most important of the islands in those early days, yet now only two churches have been left standing, both of which date from that period. It is a place that has returned to its natural state. The cathedral of Santa Maria Assunta and the small church of Santa Fosca are both unlikely remnants of the Venetian-Byzantine style of the eleventh and twelfth centuries (although the former also contains elements from the seventh century) and of a population that (unlike the Venetians themselves, whose numbers grew and then stopped growing) grew and decayed to the point where the earth swallowed up the palaces and the other churches, the monasteries and the houses, as well as a flourishing wool industry. Venice is not a true ruin, but Torcello is, the victim of its increasingly swampy waters and of malaria. In one of the mosaics inside the cathedral (the one showing the Last Judgement), there is an extraordinary depiction of Lucifer. To his right stand some spear-wielding angels busily flinging into the fires of hell those found guilty of pride, here represented by crowned and mitred heads with ermine collars and bejewelled ears. Those heads are immediately seized upon by small green angels, the fallen ones. Lucifer, seated on a throne the arms of which are the heads of dragons engaged in devouring human bodies, has the same face and is making the same gesture as God the Father; he has the same abundant white beard and hair, the same venerable appearance, his right hand raised in a gesture of greeting and of serenely imposed order. On his knees sits a pretty child all dressed in white, who looks like the Infant Redeemer,

God the Son. But Lucifer's face and body are dark green: he is a topsy-turvy version of God the Father, or, rather, a negative version, and the child sitting on his lap is the Antichrist, who also has his right hand raised in greeting – the very same gesture – like a small prince gently beckoning to the dead.

The dead in Venice have their own island too, occupying the whole of San Michele, whose walls – it is the only walled island – can be seen from the *vaporetto* as you approach. The tops of cypresses wave above the walls, warning the visitor of what awaits them. And the view from the water provides the best perspective from which to see the façade of the Renaissance church, built by that excellent architect Codussi, and made, like so many other Venetian churches, out of white Istrian stone, one of the city's colours.

The cemetery of San Michele, though, is an impersonal place. Unlike the cemeteries of Hamburg or Lisbon or Scotland, there are no large groups of monumental sculptures or inspired inscriptions, but merely descriptive notes, firmly rooted in life rather than addressed to the hereafter: 'Elizabetta Ranzato Zanon, a woman of strong character', as one can see from the relief carving of her rather grumpy face; 'Pietro Giove Fu Antonio, an honest businessman'; 'Giuseppe Antonio Leiss di Laimbourg, an expert and disinterested lawyer with a heart of gold'. One of the more elegant graves appears to contain the remains of an apocryphal Emily Brontë character: 'Gambirasi Heathcliff'. As a nod to the tourists, there are arrows on which appear three names: 'Stravinsky, Diaghilev, Pound'. The first two are in the Greek section, where the composer lies beside his wife, Vera, their identical graves bearing only their names picked out in black-and-blue mosaic. They are very distinguished tombs, rather enviable, made from white marble and edged in red granite. On each tomb lie three withered carnations, which make me think of poor Schubert's possibly fake tomb in Vienna, surrounded now by a garden. Far too many famous people have passed through Venice, and Pound's grave, for example, is now a green mound bearing only his name, lost in the middle of the rarely visited and much neglected evangelical area, where twisted fragments of fallen

crosses have impaled the gravestones themselves. It's almost impossible to find Pound's
grave among the undergrowth. No one repairs
the damage wrought by a recent storm. In the
summer, the only visitors to the dead of San
Michele are the lizards, no one else. Who in
Venice would have time to tend the graves
of these foreign dead, of the vanished lives of
these visitors? Foreigners die here more defini-
tively. Perhaps that's why they keep coming, to
tempt fate.

The point of view
of eternity

In Venice, perhaps fortunately, there are only
one or two paintings by Canaletto. Nearly everything he produced is to be found in Britain
thanks to Consul Joseph (or Giuseppe) Smith
(1674-1770), who spent forty-four years in the
city before being honoured with that diplomatic
title, although, in fact, he brought far more
honour to the title than it did to him. As a fabu-
lously wealthy trader in fish and meat and as
one of the greatest art collectors of his day,
Consul Smith lived for seventy of his ninety-six
years in Venice, most of them in the Palazzo
Mangilli-Valmarana, on the corner of the
Grand Canal and Rio dei Santi Apostoli. He had
more than enough time during those seven
decades to gather together various collections
of paintings, sculptures, musical instruments,
scores, manuscripts, books, engravings, coins,

cameos, medals and jewels, which he later sold for exorbitant prices to the Crown of England; he also sponsored and promoted many artists, among them the Ricci brothers, Zuccarelli, Rosalba Carriera and, of course, Canaletto. Of the latter's work – and this is why so little of it can be found in Venice – Consul Smith managed to sell virtually everything and even dispatched the painter to work in London for ten years. Every wealthy English visitor wanted to take home some visual souvenir of his stay in the city, and what more appropriate, reliable or exact souvenir could there be than a view by Canaletto? His paintings were the equivalent of postcards for those pioneering tourists, the English aristocrats who always included Venice in their Grand Tour.

But although the present-day visitor will see few Canalettos and will have to make do with reproductions or with memories, he will see many Venetian landscapes from the same period, by Guardi, Marieschi, Carlevaris, Bellotto, Migli-ara, in the city's various museums. And yet, as I said earlier, perhaps it's fortunate that there are virtually no Canalettos, those precise, detailed, almost photographic records, because the views you get in the paintings of those eighteenth-century *vedutisti* are, astonishingly, exactly the same as those you will see on emerging from the Galleria dell'Accademia or Ca' Rezzonico or Museo Correr. This strange sensation produces an equally strange mixture of euphoria and unease. And the truth is that those feelings are only intensified if you have also seen certain paintings by Gentile Bellini, Mansueti or Carpaccio. For you discover that nothing has changed, not just in two hundred and fifty years, but in almost five hundred. The canvases from the cinquecento will show almost the same views as were painted in the settecento; and in the novecento, you stagger, exhausted, out of the museums, only to be confronted by the same scenes outside. The biggest change will doubt-less be the people and their clothes: aristocrats and clerics, black bonnets, long hair, Renais-sance cloaks, tight red, white or striped hose in Bellini and Carpaccio; artisans and members of the bourgeoisie, wigs, waistcoats, masks, Sat-urn hats and loose shirts in Carlevaris or Guardi; crowds of tourists and hideous Bermuda shorts

23

or T-shirts bearing slogans in the streets outside. Everything else, everything non-human,
remains the same.

The visitor knows this beforehand, and to
some degree it is precisely this 'archaeological'
aspect of the city that has impelled him to travel
here. And yet it's still impossible not to be a little
surprised when you stop and think about it, or if
you try the simple experiment of looking at a
couple of paintings and then at your surround-
ings. Venice is the only city in the world whose
past you do not have to glimpse or intuit or guess
at, it's there before you, at least its past appearance is, which is also its present appearance.
Even more exciting and disquieting is the fact
that the city's present appearance is also the
city's future appearance. Looking at Venice
now, not only do you see it as it was one hundred,
two hundred and even five hundred years ago,
you see it as it will be in one hundred, two hundred, probably even five hundred years' time.
Just as it is the only inhabited place in the world
with a visible past, so it is also the only one with
its future already on display.

There has been some construction work - a

few houses in the more working-class areas, the new headquarters of the Cassa di Risparmio in Campo Manin (the work of the famous architect Pier Luigi Nervi in 1963), the Previdenza Sociale, the Mussolinian railway station and a few others – but, apart from that, you could say that all building ceased in Venice before its current inhabitants were born. And you can, above all, be quite sure that nothing will be built, unless one of the houses were to be destroyed by some unforeseen event, leaving a gap for the architects of the present and the future to fill.

It's rather touching to think that, despite this, Venice has her own twentieth-century architectural genius in Carlo Scarpa (1906–78), who was born here. Scarpa's case is significant though; his wonderful, instantly recognizable works are, in Venice, reduced to mere details, but he is nevertheless revered by his fellow Venetians, who live among the most perfect collection of architectural monuments in history; they go into raptures over the Olivetti Showroom in St Mark's Square, the doors of the faculties of Architecture or Literature, the old lecture hall (restored by him) in Ca' Foscari, the staircase in

Casa Balboni or the courtyard of the Fondazione Querini Stampalia. In each of these, there might be four steps to admire, or a roof or a door or a radiator grille. That is what the work of the great Carlo Scarpa consists of in his native city. No one can touch Venice, and he was no exception. Venice is the city with the clearest idea of its own future, and that is why perhaps the past - the immense, omnipresent, overwhelming weight of the past - is never set against an identical and already known future, but against the threat of disappearance.

Ever since my first visit to Venice in 1984, I have been back twice or more each year. Now, I may be wrong, but I have always had the sense that the threat of catastrophe, of irremediable calamity or total annihilation, was less a genuine fear among its inhabitants and more of a necessity. This deliberate feeling of dread - artificially created, in my view - immediately infects visitors too, probably even the most ephemeral ones, who have only to set foot on a bridge to feel that this could well be the city's final day.

Venice is the most protected and studied city

in the world, the most closely monitored and watched. The universal desire is not only to preserve it, but to preserve it exactly as it is now. We know that it cannot cease to exist, that it cannot be lost. Probably not even a world war would permit that. The terrible certainty that something we can actually see will always be there and will always remain the same, without the admixture of unease and uncertainty inherent in all human enterprises and communities, without the possibility of a new life or of an unprecedented rebirth, of growth or expansion, without the possibility, in short, of any surprise or change, means that Venetians see life from 'the viewpoint of eternity'. That is the phrase used by Mario Perez who, despite his name (without an accent on the first 'e'), is one of the few people born, raised and still living in Venice whom it has been my privilege to know. The viewpoint of eternity! The words froze my blood while we were having supper together: I was eating sole, and he salmon. Can there be a more frightening, unbearable, less human point of view?

I suppose the only way of making that certainty and that viewpoint bearable is to give in to the temptation of believing in the imminent destruction of what will doubtless survive us, and to foster the threat and fear of total extinction. Each time I arrive in Venice, I find the population alarmed about something or other, be it an old threat or a new. Sometimes it's stone decay, which is corroding the city faster than in past centuries; sometimes it's the backpackers and the excessive number of *pendolari* (day-trippers, of whom there can be as many as thirty thousand daily); at others it's the *acqua alta*, when the tide is unusually high and overflows into the lower parts of the city (starting with St Mark's Square), ruining shopkeepers, requiring benches to be put together to form improvised mini-bridges in the streets, and causing terrible flooding, as happened on 4 November 1966, that disastrous day when the water rose more than six feet, leaving everything stained with damp and caked in salt for months afterwards; the city is, of course, slowly sinking, at the rate of about six inches a century, they say; the nearby industries have succeeded in corroding the stone in only a matter of years, far more quickly than in any of the previous, far less productive centuries; and there is always the possibility that an earthquake might transform Venice into a vast, labyrinthine underwater palace (years ago, minor tremors caused some of the smaller islands in the estuary to vanish).

One of the more recent threats has been the proliferation of algae in the bottom of the lagoon, together with a plague of Chironomidae, insects that resemble clumsy mosquitoes and sometimes form such dense clouds that they blacken windows or force trains to stop and planes to abandon take-off. The detritus from the factories in neighbouring Marghera acts like a fertilizer on the algae, which grows and reproduces so fast that four boats scooping up thousands of tons of the stuff day and night haven't been enough to clear the lagoon bed. The algae rots in the boiling summer heat. The fish die and float on the surface as if they were the water's unexpected, multiple gaze. And depending which way the wind is blowing (or even if there is no wind at all), a smell of pestilence takes over the city. It's the all-enveloping stench of putrefaction. The fetid odour wakes you in the middle of the night, and whereas in any other place this would be assumed to be a temporary phenomenon, in Venice, you some-how imagine it will be perpetual, global, a state of mind, a clear sign that the end of civilization is nigh. These perhaps are the disadvantages of living life from the viewpoint of eternity.

The night stroll

Apart from going to see the things you feel obliged to see and which are never-ending, the only diversion in Venice in August is to walk and look and walk and look. Not that there's very much more to do in winter, apart, now and then, from the occasional concert or, under the auspices of Agnelli, a new exhibition hung on the pink-tinged walls of Palazzo Grassi.[1] In fact, the only thing Venetians have in common with their former invaders, the Austrians, is their passion for music. Concerts are the one event for which you cannot find tickets, and among the few moments that remain fixed in the homogenizing memory of Venice's inhabitants is the night, for example, when the pianist Sviatoslav Richter stopped time (and this in a place where time

1 At the time this was written, the interior walls of Palazzo Grassi were painted a shade of pink.

stands still anyway) with the second movement of a Haydn sonata at La Fenice. But then, in August, everything grinds to a halt, and for those citizens and tourists who don't want to see one of the movies being shown on the giant open-air screen erected in Campo San Polo and who aren't too worn out by their daytime wanderings, by the heat or by Stendhal syndrome – which claims many victims here – their only option will be to walk and look.

The city changes completely at night. It's one of the liveliest cities I know during the day, but when the sun sets, everything disappears or closes, and as the hours pass, Venice becomes ever more deserted and ever more the province of individual noises. The sound of footsteps is intercut with the slap of water, and almost any corner of the city looks even more like a stage-set than usual, given that a set never looks quite so set-like as when it's empty. But what really changes Venice is the darkness itself. At night – this is the complaint of many of the biblical hordes of tourists – it's barely lit at all, apart from the occasional church or palace on the Grand Canal. Along the minor canals and backstreets, which constitute the real city, there is only perhaps a street lamp here, a lantern there, the occasional miserly crack of light between those watermelon-green shutters. There are places where the darkness is almost total, and you can stand on a bridge for hours vainly trying to make out anything more than the mere outline of buildings and the invisible flow of water. Water is the city's fundamental element. By day, it reflects and intensifies the light and colour (blood red, yellow, white) of the houses and the palaces. By night, though, it reflects nothing. It absorbs. On moonless nights – last night, for example – it's like ink, and so seems much more stagnant than it actually is. Then the only real illumination comes from the buildings made of that intensely white Istrian stone: Santa Maria della Salute or the Palazzo Mocenigo Casa Nuova; San Giorgio Maggiore or Il Redentore, seen from the Zattere.

The walker who fears getting lost in the gloomier corners of the city, but fancies a lengthy stroll along a spacious promenade by the water, has two options: Riva degli Schiavoni or the Zattere. The first, which begins at St

Mark's Square, will be popular with those who require some continuity of appearance between different places. There, in Schiavoni, they will still find people, possibly too many: the hustle and bustle of street-sellers, crowds of young people, Japanese and Spanish, standing around the obelisks, restaurants and bars, although few of the latter will remain open past midnight. The extremely bronzed waiter at the Bar do Leoni, who was filing his nails at mid-afternoon in readiness to welcome customers exhausted by fatigue and ecstasy, will already be putting the chairs back on the tables. A little further east, the endless lines of moored *motoscafi* are rocked by the coming and going of the lagoon waters, producing, as they do, an extraordinary symphony of metallic squeaks and bumps that must be a torment to the inhabitants of the old people's home opposite. There are still crowds in Riva degli Schiavoni, but they are a spent force. Only Harry's Bar, a short distance in the opposite direction, will proudly continue to be full of life, with its gallery of well-dressed characters and its American families following in the footsteps of the blessed Hemingway. Its small legendary dining room, preserved intact since 1931 by the Cipriani family, is definitely the best restaurant in the city, and a meal there is something that should be afforded even by those who really can't.

But the other long *fondamenta*, or walkway, that takes you past broad stretches of water (in the Grand Canal there are only short sections that are passable) are the so-called Zattere (meaning, literally, rafts). The Zattere run along the southernmost edge of the city, from which you can contemplate the island of La Giudecca, separated from Venice proper by a wide canal of the same name, so wide and deep that ships sail down it. The extraordinary Fondamenta delle Zattere is well known but somewhat hidden and will be found only by those, for example, who, after visiting the church of Santa Maria della Salute, go as far as the end of the Dogana, the old Customs House, and then turn back on themselves. Unlike the Riva degli Schiavoni, it is silent and fairly solitary. Now and then you might encounter a café terrace where a few of the city's inhabitants and a handful of well-informed visitors are enjoying a quiet drink or an ice cream, but otherwise there are only long stretches of stone pavement, to one side of which is a wall and to the other water, although the wall is now and then interrupted by a low bridge beneath which flows a *rio*, or minor canal, pointing the way back into the heart of Venice.

On the other side of the Canale della Giudecca, you can see the island, with the Palladian Chiesa del Redentore lit up, and further east, greatly foreshortened, on its own island, the church of San Giorgio Maggiore, also designed by Palladio. The walker must then turn his back on that and start crossing bridges: Ponte dell'Umiltà, Ponte Ca' Balà, Ponte agli Incurabili. The only thing approaching a crowd you are likely to meet is a couple who have perhaps reached the Zattere by chance or on a whim and are standing on a bridge, unsure which way to go next, or perhaps watching one of the big ships passing, and which has suddenly become a moving part of La Giudecca. Since both buildings and ships in Venice are on a level with the water, and since the buildings are never more than two or three or four storeys at most, they can easily disappear behind a large vessel, and there are

36

moments when a Russian or Dutch or Greek ship completely supplants the Chiesa del Redentore or Chiesa delle Zitelle, as if in a scene from a Hitchcock film, erasing them from our vision for a few seconds. You come across children too, fishing for squid and plaice with nets. '*Una seppia e sette passarini*,' says one small bespectacled child, when I ask him what's in his plastic bag. Meanwhile, a lizard escapes along the wall to my right. After the next bridge, della Calcina, there is a plaque commemorating John Ruskin, 'the high priest of art', to whom, according to the inscription, 'every marble, every bronze, every painting, every thing cried out'. This inconsiderate cacophony might go some way to explaining the more hysterical passages in that high priest's *Stones of Venice*.

Further on, past the Ponte Lungo and towards the west, as you approach the Stazione Marittima and the end of the Zattere and the walk itself, you see the most amazing sight of all. During the day, to the west, you can make out the industrial complexes of neighbouring Marghera, but what we're interested in lies straight ahead, where La Giudecca ends. Looming out of

the darkness on the other side stand two buildings of a Nordic or Hanseatic appearance; they
are tall and square and one of them is a colossal
seven storeys high, something you never see in
Venice. The larger of the two is a colourless
hulk. Shortly before you reach them, the waters
of La Giudecca are still reflecting the bright
lamps outside Harry's Dolci, another establish-
ment belonging to the Cipriani empire. There,
however, beneath those Nordic hulks – like a
chunk of Hamburg or Copenhagen – the water is
blacker than at any other point, there's not even
a security guard's flashlight of a light left on by
some insomniac. There are no Gothic windows,
no Renaissance mouldings, no white Istrian
stone, not a trace of red, just a dark, gloomy,
derelict, nineteenth-century construction: this
is Molino Stucky, the vast flour factory erected
in 1884 despite many protests, and which has
stood empty since the Second World War. So far,
no new purpose has been found for it that
would justify its restoration, its return to life.
The waiter in the restaurant opposite eyes
these 'modern' buildings scornfully and tells me
that they're completely deserted apart from

'*pantegane come gatti*' (which means 'rats as big as cats'). This mass of iron, brick and slate, the one factory to be built within the city's confines, rises up, decayed and austere, like a trophy won by Venice itself, that paradise of the unnecessary and the useless, with its back turned haughtily on the present. Everything unnecessary and useless, everything that can only be walked past and looked at, remains alive, sometimes escaping ruin by a hair's breadth. In the unnecessary and useless there is always a light, however faint, even if its sole purpose is to illuminate the surrounding gloom, as Faulkner once said about striking a match in the darkness. Molino Stucky, however, lies in permanent darkness, and the walker along the Zattere, across the water, will struggle to guess the past of that emblematic tower and pinnacle, those futile walls and blind windows, a far less distant, but less decipherable, past than that of any palazzo.

The imaginary space

You could walk from the west to the east of Venice (which is the longest possible distance) in about an hour, at a brisk pace and without getting out of breath. But almost no one does this: firstly, because it's difficult, if not impossible, to follow a relatively straight line without pausing a hundred times en route; and, secondly, because of what we, rather pedantically, might call its 'endless imaginary fragmentation'.

Venice provokes two simultaneous and apparently contradictory feelings: on the one hand, it is the most homogeneous – or, if you prefer, harmonious – city I have known. By homogeneous or harmonious I mean that any point in the city that enters the observer's field of vision, any luminous open space or secret misty corner, with water or without, could only possibly belong to this one city, could never be confused with any other urban landscape or evoke memories of elsewhere; it is, therefore, the very opposite of anodyne. (With the possible exception of Lista di Spagna, that stretch of street which, to the great confusion and misfortune of many visitors arriving by train, is the first thing one sees; it is best, therefore, to jump on a *vaporetto* or immediately cross the bridge.)

On the other hand (and herein lies the contradiction), few cities seem more spread out and more fragmented, full of insuperable distances and places that feel utterly isolated. Venice is divided into six *sestieri*, or quarters: San Marco, San Polo, Cannaregio, Santa Croce, Dorsoduro and Castello. Even within each *sestiere* there are areas that seem a world away from any other, even the world that is not only next door, but adjacent and contiguous.

This feeling is not entirely false, insofar as it's not exclusive to the visitor, who, unfamiliar with the city's meandering streets, might miscalculate and think that he set off from his starting point earlier than he actually did; rather, it has deep roots in the inhabitants of Venice themselves, and I am not referring, as I

42

did earlier, only to the most powerful, to the movers and shakers (although never have I known movers and shakers move or shake less), but to the ordinary inhabitants, shopkeepers, the few remaining craftsmen, housewives, and, of course, children, who, here as elsewhere – unlikely as it may seem – have to go to school. Mario Perez tells me that he knows a lady who, like him, lives in Castello, but who has never once set foot in St Mark's Square; now and then she asks him how things are going over there in the same tone of voice in which she might inquire about events in Madagascar or some other remote place from which he had just returned after a long voyage, bearing fresh news. This 'imaginary' distancing is a condition of existence in Venice: you live mainly in the restricted world of the street, the canal or the quarter, and the totality of Venice (and therein lies its harmony and homogeneity) is perceived only in fragments, albeit perfectly articulated. The Venetians are, of course, the ones most keenly aware of this fragmentation and articulation, but the astonishing thing is that, intuitively and possibly with no need for it to be put into words, this awareness instantly takes root in visitors as well, however transient and unobservant they may be. And it is doubtless this intuited notion that forbids them – if I may put it so – from entering many parts of the city, into which they will never venture even if the map is telling them that they are only a step away.

Perhaps they're right not to take risks. The more adventurous visitor might reach Campo dell'Anconetta heading towards Strada Nova, very close to the Grand Canal, which will always serve him as the city's axis. Suddenly, seduced by curiosity or by the desire to see a particular church, he might turn left and cross no fewer than three canals – Rio della Misericordia, Rio della Sensa, Rio della Madonna dell'Orto – and find himself in front of the superb church bearing the latter name. And the five minutes it took him to get there might be enough to give him the strange impression that he is a thousand leagues from the Grand Canal. Having studied the ten Tintorettos in that church and the beautiful Bellini Virgin depicting a lunatic Christ Child who looks as if he's either going to choke to death at any moment or pounce on his extraordinary mother, the visitor will doubtless retrace his steps and be astonished to find how close he was to something that was clearly far away while he was wandering beside those secondary canals, because he really *was* far away.

Space in Venice should be measured by state of mind and character and by the *idea* that emanates from each *sestiere*, each quarter, each canal and each street, not by the number of yards separating them. For example, the same person seen in different places will vary, even though his function or activity is the same in all of them. There is in Venice a beggar (oddly enough, despite all those tourists, you don't see many, which is why they're easy to recognize) who begs for alms in all six *sestieri*. He's rather chubby and getting on in years; he wears a hat that is a tad too small for him, plays the panpipes – an instrument that betrays his southern origins – and displays to the compassionate gaze of passers-by a pale, plump plastic calf that emerges from a very short white sock. It is the cleanest leg I have ever seen, and I always stop to look at it. I give

45

him a few coins to reward such cleanliness as well as the pleasant sound of his pipes. This eminently recognizable man, however, is quite different depending on whether he's in San Marco, San Polo, Cannaregio, Santa Croce, Dorsoduro or Castello. In the first of those *sestieri*, he seems like a fraud or a local con man preying on tourists; in the second, his 'foreign' *terrone* aspect seems more pronounced and he looks out of place; in the third, he blends in so well that no one even notices that he's begging for alms with his impeccable leg. It's the setting that dictates how things appear, and so it isn't the same seeing a tourist crossing the Rialto Bridge as it is seeing him crossing one of the various Ponti delle Tette. These are the darkest and most hidden, the least touristy of bridges, offering the most limited views, and their name arises from the fact that they were the only bridges on which the Doge would allow the impoverished streetwalkers of the eighteenth century to show their tits – or *tette* – to the passers-by and thus attract more clients, who were apparently too distracted at the time by the exquisite courtesans arriving from all over

46

Europe and by a prevailing fashion for homo-
sexuality.

In Venice, though, each fragment is a whole.
Sometimes the streets are so narrow and tortu-
ous that we can see very little, yet a fragment,
any fragment, will form a momentary whole,
and will be unmistakably Venice. There is nothing more instantly identifiable or more complete
than the little San Trovaso *squero*, or dry dock,
for gondolas, a tiny wooden construction (wood
for once, not stone) next to which a few vessels
lie waiting in the dark to be repaired: for the
gondolas, which, as I mentioned before, are the
perfect height from which to view the city (even
the *vaporetti* are too high in the water), continue to have a function and a life and can still be
restored, unlike the Molino Stucky. From an
arcade behind La Fenice, you can see the glau-
cous waters of the Rio Menùo, a scrap of pink
palace, a large door painted in the usual water-
melon green, and a few steps. From where I am
writing, I can see the pillars of my balcony, the
Rio delle Muneghette, two boats, the shop selling toy windmills, and the Scuola di San Rocco
in the background. There are people who will

have spent a lifetime seeing only the San Trovaso dock or that fragment of the Rio Menùo or this view from my terrace, just as the old lady in Castello, whom Mario Perez told me about, hasn't once set foot in St Mark's Square.

Venice is a *hypercity*. Perhaps the smug Venetians who insist that everything else is mere *campo* are, after all, right. There are no exteriors, here everything is stone, everything is built, the gardens you can see from the top of the Campanile are nowhere to be found when you wander through Venice: they are private, enclosed, and belong neither to the walker nor to the general population. Yet there need be nothing artificial about one's relationship with this place of stone, as the panicky, harassed tourists believe, who mistakenly travel here in an exclusively cultural spirit. When I call Venice a *hypercity* or, as Venetians would have it, the City par excellence, I mean, above all, that in the minds of the people who love it, it is those things necessarily and naturally, and perhaps not as deeply cultured as you might think, but at once instinctive and not in the least accidental. A city like this can be natural without, at the

48

same time, owing anything to chance. Perhaps there is another way of understanding and describing it. According to Daniella Pittarello, an Italian from Padua who has lived here for ten years: 'Venice is an interior.' And she adds that it is precisely because there is no *outside* and because it is complete in itself, that it can be so difficult, albeit necessary sometimes, to leave, just as it gets harder and harder to leave home when you haven't done so for a long time. Henry James saw it in a very similar way: 'where voices sound as in the corridors of a house, where the human step circulates as if it skirted the angles of furniture and shoes never wear out . . .' To say that Venice is an interior is a possible summation of everything I have said so far. It means that it is self-sufficient, that it has no need of anything outside itself and that this same self-sufficiency is what creates that 'endless imaginary fragmentation': the narrow becomes wide, the near becomes far, the limited becomes infinite, the identical becomes distinct, the timeless becomes transient.

The things we
carry with us

Between December 1984 and October 1989 – for personal reasons I need not go into here – I flew to Venice fourteen times, from Spain and from England and, on one occasion, from the United States. My stays in the city varied in length from the hectic four days of my first visit to the seventy days of my longest visit; and during that five-year period, I spent, in all, a total of nine months in Venice, long enough for me to feel it was a place in which I partially lived, my second – ever-present – city, to which I went and from which I returned, and to which I always thought I would go back. There I wrote a good part of my novels *The Man of Feeling* and *All Souls*, and my day-to-day Venetian life was nothing like that of a tourist, or even of a traveller. I fitted into the routine of the people who so generously took me in, two women, both called Daniela, who shared a house. In order to distinguish them, I would address one as Daniela plus her surname and the other as Daniella, with two 'l's. Since they both worked and had to go out early and I had more time at my disposal, I was left in charge of washing the dishes (rather inexpertly), doing the shopping and running various other domestic errands. Indeed, I had time enough to write those two novels and to stroll about the city on my own, always aimlessly, slowly, calmly, just seeing what I might come across, without any of the haste of normal visitors and the programme of visits they set themselves when they have only a few days in which to get to know a city. At one point, I came very close to settling down there, and had even found myself a job. I didn't know that my fourteenth visit would be my last, or, rather, I didn't know that twenty years would pass before my next visit.

When you have lived for a while in a city, especially if it has proved to be an intense experience and happens to coincide with one of those ages so crucial in most people's lives (between the ages of thirty-three and thirty-eight in my case), regardless of how much time passes, you never stop thinking about that place. You carry it around with you, it becomes part of you, and I often have the strange feeling that I could leave my apartment in Madrid, or anywhere else, and head straight for some particular spot in that distant city, to a church, a shop, a square, to the Zattere or San Trovaso if it's Venice, to St Giles or Blackwell's if it's Oxford, or to Cecil Court or Gloucester Road if it's London. It didn't feel as if twenty years had passed since my last stay there, and yet they had, almost half a lifetime, if you like. We live in a reality that is very different from the past and we certainly don't lose touch with that reality when we receive a sudden visitation from the distant past. However, as I've often said before, space is the only true repository of time, of past time. And that is why, when you go back to a familiar city, time undergoes a brief, sudden compression, and what was far away in Madrid the day before yesterday becomes spuriously close in Venice today. After a first few hesitant steps, those same steps automatically take you along routes you had apparently forgotten the day before, and which you suddenly remember. Almost without thinking, you say: you have to go down there to reach such-and-such a place and to reach so-and-so you head in that direction, and you never get lost or go wrong. There, before me, was the house to which I once had the key, the address was San Polo 3089; I can't go in there now, not just because I no longer have a key, but because the two Danielas no longer live there. Sitting on the steps that separate the water – Rio delle Muneghette – from the back of the Scuola di San Rocco that I used to see from the balcony where I would stand when taking a break from writing those two, now old, novels, I smoke a cigarette and look across at the house and that balcony. The house used to be white, but its new owners have painted it an orangey-pink colour, yet I say to myself: that's the house, I'm sure of it, I spent many an evening and afternoon there; on many nights, I slept there; I would get up in the morning and look out at the water and at the steps on which I'm sitting now, twenty years later.

Fortunately, Venice is barely allowed to change at all, and the barges full of fruit are still there next to Campo San Barnaba, where I would do my somewhat inexpert food-shopping; the church of Santi Giovanni e Paolo is still there, in a square scorned by tourists and which, in any other city, would be its crowded centre. And, to my great good fortune, the people are still there too, and I've made my peace with them. I had supper one night with the two Danielas and with Cristina; they had barely changed, as if they had made a pact with some minor, rather inoffensive devil. Suddenly, in their company, it wasn't that time hadn't passed for each of us (far from it: they've all been married, one is divorced and the other is in the process of getting divorced, one has daughters, another moved to Florence, but came back to Venice especially to see me), but our talk and our laughter were, implausibly, just the same, at least for a while, as it used to be when we were young. It's always very cheering to find there are people and places that are always there, even though they're far away or seem to have been lost. We probably only really lose what we forget or reject, what we prefer to erase and no longer wish to carry with us, what is no longer part of the life we tell ourselves.

Author's note

Though it is said in this text that Venice never changes, that is inaccurate of course, as all places suffer some changes, even if slight ones. It must be noted that *Venice, An Interior* was written in 1988, when, to give just an example, Molino Stucky was the derelict building here alluded to, and not the present-day hotel it has become.

Venice, An Interior is extracted from the forth-coming collection of non-fiction writing by Javier Marias, *Between Eternities*, translated by Margaret Jull Costa and edited by Alexis Grohmann.